**RENTAL VAN**

**DATE DUE**

| | | | |
|---|---|---|---|
| | | | |
| | | | |
| | | | |
| | | | |
| | | | |
| | | | |
| | | | |
| | | | |
| | | | |
| | | | |
| | | | |
| | | | |
| | | | |
| | | | |
| | | | |
| | | | |
| | | | |
| GAYLORD | | | PRINTED IN U.S.A. |

JAN 0 9 2008

## OTHER BOOKS BY CLINT BURNHAM

*The And that Cain Forgot*
*Allegories of Publishing: The Toronto Small Press Scene*
*Leo Lines*
*Fatal Femmes: The Poetry of Lynn Crosbie*
*The Jamesonian Unconscious: The Aesthetics of Marxist Theory*
*Pandemonia*
*Steve McCaffery and His Works*
*Be Labour Reading*
*Feminist Trilogy*
*Airborne Photo*
*Buddyland*
*Airborne Comics* (with Cory Van Ieperen)
*A4isms*
*Smoke Show*

# RENTAL VAN

## Clint Burnham

Anvil Press | Vancouver

Anvil Press Inc.
P.O. Box 3008, Main Post Office
Vancouver, B.C. V6B 3X5 CANADA
www.anvilpress.com

Library and Archives Canada Cataloguing in Publication

Burnham, Clint, 1962-
        Rental van / Clint Burnham.

Poems.
ISBN 978-1-895636-81-9

        I. Title.

PS8553.U665R45 2007        C811'.54        C2007-901760-6

Printed and bound in Canada
Cover image: Geoffrey Farmer, Courtesy Catriona Jeffries Gallery, Vancouver
Author photo: Roger Allen
Interior & cover design: HeimatHouse

Represented in Canada by the Literary Press Group
Distributed by the University of Toronto Press

The publisher gratefully acknowledges the financial assistance of the Canada Council for the Arts, the Book Publishing Industry Development Program (BPIDP), and the Province of British Columbia through the B.C. Arts Council and the Book Publishing Tax Credit.

In memory of Terry Johnson
1959 – 2004

Rental Van

2. Now where I was was whae was I
super pramits chairs med pep dunk tank
di da di
Ocular to Ocular

A.m. I.I.G.A.F.
British Props
98 Ruskin
inverted-V
O. style
HARD COP
MP Haiku
gotta kxander gumbo Itsuky galch angus lark
blah coover
Flower Dashly Haiku
I have a Third Grade Ense of Humor (Rental Van 4.1)
Poverty Pimp
Choke the Chicken Hawk Leftist
Chicken Fallujah

## 2. Now where I was was where was I

1. life and death
decisions are
a way of life
pot rattle snare
snap of window
bars fever ague
with precarious
walk up walk
see hear now
4. but gently
releasing recompense
a john cob
for mod mud
ho's is
hose 8. la's not
fair

3 how 98%
 of the people
means paranoid
what a bit
fear taken off
the e or p
if "I" had
a hammer
I'd put
it down
6. nose as not
shown and all
theyir's rubble
9. as

5. down up in
cypress hills
students as
deer caught
in headlights
out of the
parking lots
onyx night
photographic
zenophobic
7. rob ball
to pay paula
10. if

# super proximity chairs med pep dunk trank

Uptown it's too late to give the it's not too late speech. For forty more minutes Bryon who is ill with being ill about his illness which is ill not just ill at ease, ill equipped ill@ but ill (& ill@) as poems descend into email terseness. And punctuation turns out to be not just object not just just not, collapsed words the wound of @ made royal. My father an hour looks kingly under a paper crenellated sending the topics and objects as five to spontaneous as a tissue could care less. So it's time dot calmness within their spilling dottedness, the girl in her Pre JMZ or Jay Zee Marcy stat spectacle on the folks on broadway buy rap but which end or middle? Don't be afraid of meaning. Meaning. Be afraid of don't be afraid of meaning. Etc. Cities bum for the right reason: male of bundle material. Paper, money, food but food doesn't really burn does it? it roasts till it gives up the ghost, goes from fibre and grass tofu ture pencil lead. But we've it as such stock taking [why not 13 Billion in 1999] we buy low and shit lower. Give it away if you can believe lager lout lit. And that's because the shit eats up with all the other free pollution when people who can't afford to market their shit give it away. She resists her face around as if mis-spraining her neck or wrapping/unwrapping a bandage around her chin. As an hour ends she's the soldier 200 years ago with bandages wrapped around their bleeding scrambled egg and ketchup forehead. Lying in the front in Chechnya in full Cancun photo-based splendour. Some of the rich are guilty and defensive – hence journalism. The ones who don't feel guilty to into poetry, the rest complain about these would-be poets. No i'm describing the working class here, no the rulers. They're straight movers, not straight edge but straight. The project: don't make the kits stockbroker make the west end journalist feel stupid. What would that entail? As if it's so hard. The project of poetry: to one sin this. As if that makes a suffer. Who said it did. Ah, good.

Meaning comes back into the poem like Doug Round returning to a part in 1982 or 3 after getting offsales from the Red Lion Inn. It goes: You thought you'd be able to go to sleep now, but you hang out for a while before yawning stretching looking and pointing at the wall, tree, window, balcony. It's. Is this obvious enuff for you? I mean, do I have to spell it out for you. I. T. O. U. T. Is it only now most of us complain about cheap mass transportation because it looks cheap and there's too many people or has this always been the concern and always will be or some combination of those possibilties. Potato chips aren't the only thing that cause anal leakage: my nephew likes runny eggs. I keep meaning to go vote for just now but decided to check Stuart Keith Ross did at the Last Temptation in Kensington Market in 1995. He checked his messages from a (*) payphone in the middle of reading "Die a Millionaire (pronounced "diamonds in the air")" is as by now obvious – he directs attention in the poem's title to the slippage – both "oral" and of "meaning" and ideology – between the social condition – the idea of dying a millionare – dying rich, of the subjectification of richness that a millionaire is – and the effect, perhaps of that in having diamonds in the air – although unless they are still in carbon or the ground, they keep ending up being in air, never mind diamonds. – is as obvious as this commentary then becomes as a strategy. This obviousness is okay – it only applies to a limited number of readers (which is still a large number) – and thus remains to be discovered, deciding whether the foam in the glass of whisky is from soap residue – and therefore intentional, or from the whisky itself – and therefore accidental but, if read as soap would still have the effect of the abject. You can't wear give your fake fur to the museum cloakroom – they won't take it. Then: "Imperialism was just/an old, very old name for that/idea, that what you want, you by/historic process or just readiness/to travel, also 'need' – and/need is of course the sacred daughter/through which you improve, by/becoming more extensive." Knowledge acquired here fails elsewhere unless accompanied by the nurse and oxygen tent of support epistemology: inversely, knowledge acquired on the stairs to the community living room crudely rearranges the world, bit by bit. In colonized communities, poor skills can ensure the continuation of poverty pimps. Their jobs will always be there, even if they're somewhere else. It's not good to claim the moral high ground of not taking a paycheque. How do you earn a living? Sure, a funk version of "The Beat Goes On," but how about "Harper Valley PTA"? Eye candy, arm candy. Hell, where do the idaho potatoes in rap lyrics come from? If a poem is conversation where does the punctuation come from? We used children as silencers, car parts as scarves, put mouth on tailpipe or an apple. Part 7: Thins Seen in His Lifetime. The spread of advertising from communist hockey boards to the former faux-real world no longer the free world since there's any prisoners whom we'll invite to our hometown (we won't be there – there's nothing worse than turning forty in the house you live in for a year or two and your sister twenty years later it's now welfare housing, or towed down the canal to the indian reserve [and still they complain] [who can blame us] straw clogs and houses have become days off without pay and pays something you struggle to keep as steady as a girlfriend [or the other way around – never both, wouldn't neither, love's as reliable as a cheque from the government GST, like AIDS is have to stay joe blobs. Just what can you's K-ways referring to – buildings? Cultural knowledge isn't a tan appendectomy my the operation shined you taped last night to rewind slowly, the finger endlessly poking a bilious appendix back into the body of the new book. How many times do I have to tell you viruses don't kill people, tree lined inlets and a bad carving [colonial here, aboriginal here] kill people – seed the memory with a kiss spread diseases with a credit card dusted in cocaine you offer as id at the prison house of language poetry [you're not let in but wrestled taken away not baked] & someone else lives your live of wealthy inside another tradition, raising children as day comp from the desert storm tourists "Here's where the scud stud strew unused condoms on the islamic terrain, as if foil covered packages of turkey meat would, centuries later, be mistaken* for those chocolate gold "coins" you put quotation marks around, learning if a news for handwritten various manuals and electric typewriters

* MIS-SPELLED IN AN EARLIER DRAFT

– the last one memorized your writing one line at a time – and then DisplayWrite III and IV, WordPerfect 5.0, 5.1, and most recently Microsoft Word [these correspond to marriages, marxism, vegetarianism and the onset of – here it comes again as certain as em dashes – perpetual contract teaching]. People who make more money with less education are mystified. Make do write less, better, unless the opposite is true [ceaselessly memorizing the codes for curly quotation marks – macros and ctrl-alt-del sequences] at one point fringeing the thin beige edge* of the monitor casing *à la* Siskel and Ebert's intro sequences in the late 80s or Dos Passos's take on the early 80s. One of them is dead now. White out graduates from the title to the nook that it layers, not erases, and yet make it as smooth as ? to allow the overwriting that is the point of whiting out [unless it is not] – to make a surface for a point to smoothly glide over, whiting correcting at last [or not] as the click ball of the shaken white out per makes [and its thyroid throat near the tip] the exam invigilator into a subway transit guard arresting the under cover decoy sgraffitist. Part 8: And Loving Every Minute of It. Having every spy watch the opening sequences of doors closing living in a neighbourhood of sweatsuit sweat shops and mechanics in tearaways convinced that the only writers whose language I understand are my friends. Let me go back to the beginning. Uptown it's not too late to give the it's not too late speech. Living in a neighbourhood who sweatless shops from expensive faux foreign good and we produce the Rolling Stones' stagewear – tourists by the busloads come to uptown to pick up some jeans right here in Canada has convictions of my courage if you doubt oppression Robin Williams will show up on your doorstep in homophobic drag. Forge fellatio – when was the last time you sucked on a red sucker? Answer all armpit of the city ads. Water doesnt want to come up through your sock – it's prefer not to defy gravity and pay the price later, just lie on the floor with the dog hair and detritus, but if you insist on dredging up past memories i'll pick up after the pick up. Why whisky down? Cars must have a colour. "Code" for "arcade". Part 9: How to Invest in the Future. As your mother what almond is. Foe not correct her because you don't know the difference. Reflect on Paul's discussion of the apocaplypse club & what's the difference driving through the suburbs – like misunderstood streets, discussing Jennifer Lopez and Ricky Martin on *All in the Family* butt, gayness, that time Rob Reiner, who thirty years later would make a video for a jewish ceremony honouring his father that was censored but was now wearing a purse and they thought the men were whistling at Gloria and looks with your mother. A Quebecois teacher telling us he doesnt like american culture. Buy a clock on reserve the batteries' vowels with future options in five free range chickens medicine. Then you have to go down to the lag – we're respecting realty today – expecting reality – inspecting results from the labrador – to the professor who's a machine gunner in the 'cade [Perrier and Nintendo and nine eleven lawsuit]. Masculine fistique robs store with name tag still on your shirt – neuticles with more balls than brains telling you. Keep that doucher on a lease. The Kingsgate Shaft. Funky not sharp.

# di da di

while I nail trouth mouble over ex-tinct before your is just hold my hammer while
it's much better remembered remember he's in grey skater pants has down's height
bright cheeks gold benz jumped by a white stretch bell's cell cop cacophony sound
washed for the grave by american gravy lip 'n' tongue is the short version the
difference to my nailgun on semi or auto weekend if i don't O.D. on God rhyme
while doing time scarf wages we got to go up free because we're serbian get a door
in the foot mascara you constancy every bridal crypt episodes of caritas and storied
chambers of G-G-dragons the papers read SUFFERING IS YOUR FATE — EMBRACE IT
gauchos gravel saturday morning rituals? barely chargex of the linux brigade *how
many* how many to screw in a light bulb can non screwers tell rayon grey flecks of
lottery dandruff a steeple steeply bisected by a dozen tar strands heat around your
feet in indianapolis mournful obstinance there's five of a dismissed lover bars in a
row ragging pulled off socks look just her muff dancing in the air before her cpr
strawberries with bipolar II hypomania mill r&b channels
pj the populist centre dino-sours equivalent of
popular culture is my drug versus i'm high on life/air adult shit mix lick-m-aid is
mean to us there's joy to being barred to the temple said the new pornographers
your sweet hearts do you find it warm in here well there's no word assaults
assailants here anyway we havent had any accidents today peter lorre
elo and dr dre
contemplating a crime tortoise and supertramp most successful tweak dramatics
gonna get his teeth down and a new dress underpants fake nails break their fingers
every week pretend you didn't with my son in Squamish they tell her you've been
worse off

he writhes/they film/he watches/we watch
hear that okay got our emails screwed up pick up three grapes with four fingers
straw battery his tragic death
domestic dispute
as a tragic addict
some message 48 window limo rich nerds edjucate parole officer's kinner diddler
commentator ex cbgb's doorman's countering the pulp fiction illusion of you wouldn't
want someone interrupting you using on the street so shut up glamourous chocoholic
raincoats bundled w/elastic just because you look good doesn't mean you feel good
for your car second hand copy of rumours as the japanese say the dog barks put a
name to a face maschoing oh yah boy kleenex in hell linus's windex usmania i'm
his duff mincing words appropriate prostitution patrons neon banner ad 'round
the market with floods alt.country site a click from s&m to msnbc contagious
allergies rich people carry viruses bald shame the ravers neighbour E's vivaldi
period i don't want to get zipped up either
swiffer and febreeze amphibling vitnam heip van ITZNUTUYU, clay-boy spender
harley cission because a cookie's named after him he's a qualified e-fashionista
aad ONCE THE OUTSIDER
ALWAYS THE OUTSIDER
keys in the fish living in a mucilage box car ravers cawing to each other warnings
isn't a sign of good luck dedge weeping pussywillow 6-year-old headband
scrunchy cause it's uncommon Jones died today gurgling sound
ruptured tourist ex-
heterosexual
to month he drives the suv in the family the blank look of a progressive house dj
on his cd cover next to others just like him nine opposing biceps e@ons r@ro's
theory was that the direct experience of something always eluded one and could

invest [best] be experienced in retro-spect, in memory the kid takes music to
show today's youth's vacuity confess without the watching name
of more holes than an afghan paraded in pink or music to show today's today not
a Y2G crotchless panty town her high & low, N only hope now the "early,
neglected" can't deal hello it's all good whatever career path or architecture to
show feels as if world is just as far as ironically dyslexia's he can reach more of a
disability assault and capture for the rich melissa eh-all for AOL viewed how long
it will take neurologically to re and re the we are all bad actors and good thought
readers kitchen as a computer virus jerusalem pleasure
downloaded water later bottle balanced on a minivan's roof & big guys with joe
jobs clothes on hangers in bags video cameras at
choke points bridges
classic sig
of the top tea stable hugely undercelebrated mucilage again bunt clearplastic
upholstery tacks coke can smudges plasticky six months ago smell day laters tin
biggest megahit since the death of JFK jr dinosaur's over before they're back what
am I up to coconut sex what am I down to two hundred tv's never been a husband
but had plenty of wives sometimes hold my roughly four sheets stapled open to
the last page over volunteers are easier to order around twice as many to the ninth
page me later cause their media sassy the fuzzy edge of the contrails what little of
the tasters lying they decided they didn't fuck but were on the same page a note-
book on them pen in middle not Tampa Red but grant categories tv shop on tire
mipendddle men have to learn to be assholes now wait 3 days & call if it's bleeding
used to be so easy free on green tape on the vcr and works on the tv to be read
both for both even if in actuality not SHIT-DISTURBER IS A CANADIANISM you're
not a bad person just a journalist quoting karl krauss at her 'n' her henchmen
sit/smoke/wait/wait
on the cell in the truck

as good as enough except at x-raying canaries in a cage is a the coalmine keep it rooted in the present and twigged to the youth of today will never miss retro cues to get out of the way of yours the S on cotia tower rob it hotel next to it he knew it was an but: had to stop @main it's over before it starts

**2-6-00 · 3-22-00**

## Ocular to Ocular

read in
the G– U–
Supertramp's
band of the
century what
kind of country
is that he's
in the drug
dealer's sight
line but seems
like an affable
sort of guy
say send another
one he can't
get it down
behind him
the guy on his
cell in front
of the open
phone book
after saying
John V–
oh sorry
and redialling
one gang
to another

now phone
calls're
problematical
dad's voicemail's
full if you
don't have a
phone we
can't hook
up it's
his fault
he can't do
anything
about
it he
can't get
it down
then
scribble
something
in the
middle
of the book
about

lit crit
as
allegory
of
avoidance
is that
your final
the
2-man
country band
a sister
dancing
is a good
sister
hey go to
the bathroom
then he
comes back
after 20
minutes
where
were
you
at
her has
to leave
she does
shortly
after she
gets
there

R
E
N
T
A
L

# A.M.I.I.G.A.F.

morning off et
tub sox I
am the person
my parents warned me
about sparkly tan accelerator
riding the coat tails of the coat tail riders
stuck out his hand
pushing a drawer closed
full of lover's severed limbs
he ex-N.Y.
her cell the country of money
phish fans piss off ween's
toyota truck U boat & tick
took beothuk beaten track
guten tag scandal tan
things that i have put up my asshole
that i haven't put up
sarkle backpackerification
you can't call Ham
dull Saan
his suicide note in a book
as dreams lose their colour
vietnamese embroidery's
blurred edges

crisis when you realize
what you thought was objective
you had me the way
a driveway has miles on it
the world, everything in it
in exact changing
cock of leg in boot square walk
at least your day didn't start
with a barracuda movie
a bare kid in a minivan
with baseball bats
handgolf cues

dream about cars
cause you don't have a tv
dull knives
if you're not poisoned
thanks to the russian mafia
you can get local language support
for open source programs
i have been a worker three times
gas prices hikes fuels rage
already hard boiled
eggs
modificated meat loaf
lowers
's cool stamp's landing
why asking why 'N sync

R
E
N
T
A
L

                                        has to imitate
                                     millionairephilia
                                                 until
                                 keeping the porch party
                                     open for passers-by
                                    by not allowing others
                                               che chic
                                             higher state
                                      the bishop protested
                                               didn't get
                                while the getting was good
                                  blame anti-yourself forces


[early][mid][late] the
[last year]
shot gun dynasty hair model
she bolt's a nut washer
write griot shoots film and heroin
diaper landskills
shit & 3 are 9
screw & 2 makes 4 & frig makes 10
mormon board
R      capitalism's real
E      even if capital isn't
N      got a city to write
T
A
L

[pre birth][realized @
12][births][countries]
[grades]&[towns]&[houses]
[school][cities][music]

comtextsDOW OP SIT REP
mare heritage
bed dead bevy
who remembers
dittoheads U thong
exbrotherinlaw
wrecked a 3-speed
chev no longer destined
for the shah
desert tranny
panoptimist
grover or cookie monster
hanging capital Bar-Han
new landscape of face art
please leave a voice or [a] numeric

blond tinted crewcut gives the biker
a filipino rentboy look
haney hawgs jogging by          R
copshop to the 'stang ragtop    E
blood on the back of the        N
melodramatic busdriver fan's shirt  T
                                A
                                L

new cammo's gonna wake up
with a cracked skull
if he's lucky
kiss the curb

                                          I YELL BECAUSE I CARE
                                                 for tapwater tea
                    if flies fuck on a pile of shit, you know and I know who gets
                                               dirty do you think
                                          about money all the time?
                                                        We do.

UNOHUUR
it was in this period
that he used the phrase
that has since so intrigued
the philistine world
mingcourt boarded up
same celebrity scooter glitter
campbell river fishing lodge
shotgun forever

                                              what do you want darling
                                                   the waitress said
                                        2 the woman who huffed after
                                                leaving her elbows
                                               on the bar she had
                                             a ponytail on her ponytail

& pointed at the man
sitting a few tables away
see him, I
want you to hold his head
like you're about to whip
up some cake batter
in your lap and let me get
two or three orgasms
off his face

the beer label libel suit
It's on the back
I'll read it
Because that's the way things go

so like your mouth is society man
so like your mouth is society

my motherinlaw eats vegetarian
a couple times a week
the bucket of chicken
with no chicken in it

natural causes of sewage
rust around the finders
say i like rabbits
refugees with american accents
intoning the emotion
redundancy, that's it

R
E
N
T
A
L

plastic cowboyhat covers
sesame street or muppet show
let me get back to you on that
i'll be grover to your kermit

under victimless capitalism
woman in a sealy mattress
explains who casey is
to the customer
gender-repeated beatings
candy reaffirms patriarchy
when she shoots her husband

beware of B's
don't touch this wall
your son's in a coma
his wallet isn't
i went to dog classes
with my mom the other day
a fine line
between quitting
& being fired
Gerber Nak

R
E
N
T
A
L

you've got male hormones
out of date superficial references
become "historical" seaweed beard

clag heap
same statutes
same liberty
more cigarettes and meat
less buildings
a film get struck stops taxis
from stopping

had a gestaltner
winter tan & income
the photographer gets off
his scooter
takes the package off
its rack
unwraps a trophy
gives it to someone to hold
giving it to someone else
asks a woman in the back to move
takes the picture

scalpels a red rill
often opens books that way
I'm bleeding
plays on a marty
robbins vinyl
scratch repeating but there'd be
no time with a cd skip

R
E
N
T
A
L

a house of rooms
many times painted
over head-butt
wall dents

dropped salmon corpses
on trees
in late november

you will stay put
your face portrayed
back to you
in  a convex
computer screen

now repeat after me
i said i'd never
stack 3 no's in a sentence

buddhist monk
in a polarfleece vest
in a lexus
the bottom line is
I don't give a rat's ass

R
E
N
T
A
L

# British Props

shovel petals fissiparous dictionary guitar neck cup holders very different

length keep the hand

piedbald deWalt culture a test she's so on it snap-on calendar's gone tit's up

get up & change the pope's upsidedown hands

spectacles canadian literature's neighbourhood cut package illegal suites hyper trophy screw

heels into eyes kept to the forefront open to use it

my old man she rubs this ball

possible with the rise of the keyboard hold

something else inside a opium "he got for 'er" take out

inside baby

suck embarrassment affect you?

not to but to put & O'deed trashes an older least used yellow blue petal on chili oil lid version of what's he like

lightbulb cooks 3 eggs and then dope free bass jeans under white slint-eyed security

what does he like

how's the chemo King george highway's jamaican mall ask for demerol fireplace plays through kamgara with the alacrity of junkie neon?

gold ball loses backdrop foreskin pham nail walks us through carwash fishtank phamtastic as the millionaire macaroni in spaghetti car alarm in jungle cream shower apologize to the empty wheelchair would be his reasoning in

brass plate initials drawn plexi just look at watch hats off on oil tanks use brass knuckles like handcuffs and we're like 'Okay . . .' the the day after's debouched disaster 1983 tv-movie new c.o.'s a zombie

edna's poetry as source kiss coffin cosmic blowjob real world of community cultural work as the job flies out the window we learn to our chagrin paper invites are you a regular if "it's so nineties" appeared  PERSONAL perspective

from the air before or after the selection of cot and hold on trays dated

declaration of what's who dated what decade versus pre difficulty using a pen wearing a toronto's the last place i'd want to be from varaflame beer can
w/ headphones drive 'em out cigs heart tom selleck or Ian presbyterian van pulling a stump

R
E
N
T
A
L

name the north van rcmp john school

work village: nazi violence: homosexual government: greed greed: homosexual water

reflects commodities mountains reflect skyline everyone's a critic ballcap poverty is a beautiful gift hard emails muck-a-mock

daylight drivers rigid soggy fuds if you've got time to clean you've got time to lean grating ginger into a sweater ray we are history a lot

S a couple years before I met him again is there still a safeway in kerrisdale? proust's weedwhacker don't knock your bin pinched worldviews can be treated with the proper exposure the canon of Western literature wanna knuckle drag know how to kow-tow to toe cow's non-align

Is the student King Lear or is she Antigone? If your shit is wack just wear your shit can go these three questions, bum punch drunked d&d lyin' piss on li's joist 36 chambers of pot

represent computer effects in a she threw her back out carrying books why monks kept xerox & seminal sticky note stand-in for the perplexed secretary lads rarely in the morning
how change was dealt passively
stop being exploited by the church food bank anti double dipper database
a found card of hands seminarianal
it's all urine re: eating this text the opening's closed reading the words "reading this text" contribute to the alienation of the already disenfranchised

care more for a gallery than a salary hence do not feel it hard paper soft disk the light seeping through an email from someone's palmpilot

how does their missing vowel novels only became radio as our memory

I hear a song ending I think . . .

# 98Ruskin

large attendance at smart
bridge
the london grill
they are four square, to to
speak
sending a silent challenge
to the sweet enemy
mount pleasant methodist
pussy willow popular couple
respectively fashioned with
russian lace
shaugnessy Gulf clubs officers
the war has something to do
with it
great power for good in the
army

i heard a beautiful young
woman complain
just because she is a woman
illustrating two thousand of his
officers
Miss Shillabeer
destroying millions of dollars
of opium
a bouquet of lovely daffodils
we had the materials
the metals the clay the wood
trained artistic brains
turned into
valuable and marketable com-
modities

for benefit of tourists
collision of arabia maru and
tug nanoose
the light colonel's white ring
they sure had it
there are picnics and picnics
picnic's are all alike in one
respect
everyone has a good time
many novel competitions
killed by his henhouse trap
grayling's collar

# inverted-V

she well, did if

**not she's sleep such**

in an her extremely

bed beautiful last

tomato

night. perhaps – Mr. Yeah

this looked like
something ended in
a hundred-foot circle

# I insisted the Cad more

# gaz

Well that sounds pretty
that you have clarified

# an opaque underthing
## under the thing

# 0. style

He's too white to be an albino

cycles up dix street acid ecstasy we

don't call him sir he's married & his parents work for a living

o purse cam eat my fist

whitey fails want to play a hate man?

playing the car like a mandolin

One fine Sunday brunch at a hotel in the harbour, drinking Mimosa's & the trumpet player's panama hat & 4-button linen suit no stage over the half hour adieu holding americans of goodbye sold-on farewell

lying, new; dunder: the – yupper. Roo' movie [stars teeves/

teefs

omen shrooms well, not an advertizing copywriter, that's for sure over this poem a cursor that's a dated technology by the time you read this irregular arugula black dracula bitch listens to "super nigger" passing a bus end plastered with the face large al purdy poem on the skytrain hooters contest and hills because he

cooks integrates this with his life in the new male paradigm of tell your shrink
slowly do the paperwork get your consent out of the way before we get started
he loves me he loves you not don't answer the question

call mat dot

see incest rape movies with a family member shot answer anti-walker evans
*Deliverance's* floating white subjectivity New Jersey from *Paterson* to through the
lapper's Rex as window he takes the wheel & has insurance – mafia socialism.

# HARD COP

## did

you find it difficult to live to whatever that was I think these people want can't
remember his face to see you woody
kinda funny too her coat was shunned a half-highball granted we were going to
listen to stereo how did he know what the 80s
were like in 1982 yeah but being inaccurate is okay call redness lipstick put on in
the decalled newshour van no hard cop's purple slushy creeping *kitsilano-ization*
Khahtsahlano put the phone together Verner Van Dervish mix ed english von wort
dirker semi-hundred dish spare one what
are you up to sacked by bled beard moment so with you stay so trying to fuck
with me 18 in the pick up fresh haircut & a Kappa jacket greengarbagebagsuitbag
Labatts Copper boulder dropped on his truck exhaust pipe outside the free
zone you're a damn good man sister guy G warts talkative man MF represents
a false symbol of
history – looting etc
but <u>false</u> grunt probably meant yes wont doesn't gush what do you want me to do
learn to stutter still amiable though his face was wooden buns
thinks the bible isn't allowed at the U sparkle eyeshadow can you believe that
victim of a struggle to gaze how far

# YEAH

# YEAH

would you go to be popular oh and the grey camel his mother's 2 bags limping ski-
boots well where to I start you about intelectual [*sic*] socseed coladge Jug to I hope
a talk show about resumes why my mother always lost at *Scruples* they take super-
market tabloids seriously illegals for granted hi harry hibbs Kojak
Newfie leathers buried a glock cracks egg on her
worried he isn't being followed friend called her up & askedly if she wanted a
shot gun shows I'm the only lead he has they think of their datebook
testifying at her

own rape trial # don't

# worry she'll get

# you in her

# very
# legal

# get

# your

# bible tell the boy

it's a good lie

find so if other one might ho-bag last time I saw something like that I bagged it
tagged it and stuck it on my hood – rag you've been digging up in it last night
I'm not into that like that mikes under dresses everytime you kiss him you're
tasting my pussy people you think are connected but aren't pick carfluff jesus
country country out of mom's chapstick use it thickly chainsaw hands off say it
then do it dust to be bloody flapping vandalism painted
a portable burned outhouse cedar corner little memory etc don't learn lack of
cognitive ability & this is historical 2 biz cards youth leatherworker scratchitti

big

eye

girl

plaque

display

metanoia kid in respite dealer in treatment use w/ manly death & job interview
authentic soap dispenser men of quality arent checked by women seeking equality
if we get too old for sex we can hire consultants

# those
# big
# freeways
# in
# l.a.
# had
# nothing

on
the
mess
of
cars
in

# the
# drained
# out
# bathtub grandparents'

foggy trailerpark hey're hooped beertapgun somewhere in brazil growing coffee

where this dining table was

# Mp haiku

## UNTITLED

picked away blackout tape
busdriver's turban strap flattened moustache
arab frieze

bumpers land
chrome dust
cherry blossoms

Julie: off to
shoot pool w/ Mark
back 5-6 XO CB

blue green mallard's head
looks right
on the trailer hitch

## UNTITLED

styrofoam bowl
black bean soup
tarmac


## GYPSY TALKS ON IT

pavarotti's fiddle
shields
his cell phone


## WORKERBILLY

empty pop cans
top of the fridge
firehall staff room


## SNOW

armour truck
in front of the bingo hall
a dog shits
on the crosswalk

## FEBRUARY

Christmas decorations
on the porn theatre

## UNTITLED

frost on 1/2 the pillow
ahead
mattress factory fire steam

## SASHIKO

Across the river
car tops glisten
water in a frog pond

## UNTITLED

homegirl
in a Corona
mini-T

## TRANSPARENT BLUE

He had a sideburn & a
sunburn & a side arm &
drank a sidecar &
sidled up inside


## QUE + 1

microwave door
box flap side
heap in on a shopping cart
a drawing of this


## BOCCE CROWD OUTLINE NEAR THE WOMEN'S MEMORIAL[1]

on the train station lawn
old duffers kick a soccer ball
a sagging backpack


## OBLIGATORY

letter
ismilitary
ntelli
vision

R
E
N
T
A
L

# gotta lexander gumbo ltsuky gulch angus lask

Krapp you positive Tory *good day residents of vancouver!* you know what I wanna do? I wanna take a can of refried beans & remove the label & pretend like it's dogfood ou-voted better fewer but better maybe her royal social highness I'm not going to not go to work B-day office *j' en ' ccuse* of being too clever, of trying too hard, gimicks talk marks the man who knows he has the need to deceive a little thing ... and this deliberate and unconscious lack of carefulness their lives had many times depended on a diaper bib

what's the meaning of life and say listen and then there's this other thing and then you've got whatever you've got at the other end rice chaser's chick gets out of a nice italian quarter jewish quarter irish quarter lebanese nietzsche said then heidegger said then along comes the foucault trophy bio now no one's teaching sir charles g.d. roberts anymore

saw that vcrs mean jumping in with splayed feet for him well, no, jumping in with splayed feet is our middle name ugly guns is our middle name abled backers is our middle name bullshit tells money to smell whiskey and blood so so def is our middle name

use to be used to be meant he stood on top of rvs every sunday, visited land of doublewides every summer ladies let's go to that place down here what place? But you took him from me anyway and threw him away in the duff you know how your body gets so tight because it's so hungry

R
E
N
T
A
L

usually the free issue was not the *do you cappupository yourself in ten years?* issue strips away from the island for a quick unkle fucker one i don't see why i havent got the foggiest not do youth think that's a good idea?

*Norma*-like janitorial supplies Clash theme restaurant in White Rock

oh: not understanding thinking this is being ironic not hearing all of it they're being ironic no *no way, must be sitting right on top of the prop, know how? cause poop plashes diff on the radio*

I didn't say you look fat in those vintage tear-aways trop de job-y omeletteless-ness phagie, I said do you want to dance to she-beats gaiter weights there's no time to be shocked by the truth dig deep into the crates if you love her buy her a gun the beater the thieves drove across 110th street drinking iced-tea with the spoon almost cutting his nostril open unlike polanski after manson a rearview mirror in the middle of the shot butterscotch in the superstore sun way ultraboy kid accordianist digs we're trini lopez fans bigamy fokker army

somehow or other jessie's little baby brother is his father and mother's only son's need for simplicity had been drilled into them, the danger the british guy *mocks* waiting for the little white man to light up white jeep ladie's auntie's white trash with tattoos sign a gloveboxlid de-carpetwrench

effing olding money ironing your jacket before you go out weakness is pain escaping four Sturgis N.D. t-shirts yeah the woman's a bit of an asshole die come with me as though grateful for his overwhelming masterfulness glabrous coca leaves looked like a chick in the french resistance *meaning* a french collaborator chick after the war *i.e.* his her head shaved

RENTAL

very *a postiori* credit using lights rearing whisky shark on a stretcher no elbow on the door with *this* driver condom fatigue in america we don't have proverbs we have cliche's dad had the great wall of china wrapped around his foot so drunk he couldn't lie down without holding onto skipper I am a tour say together the door row the chicks click open sparring vince-arinio's big casino phobia trash is where you find it why the NRA spokesman is against fake violence guy on drywall stilts

it's easy to be monogamous on this planet cucumbers are better than anniversaries fax jokes were dated when the ink was wet my ATM etc code is 1122 a father's alive is the best he can give which is why it'll do my bowels good to see that prim British tongue lolling about when you feel that she is to [that'll] make you full capable of fronting  carp bar then she gets onto her bike when mornings are subversive famous her sac port triump of the un-unhs skills tart heart respected gesture pulling 1/2-full garbage bags up about 4 feet by the neck & then over protest jocks

hood ruled out noted the note attempt at concealment he was old in the sort of experience that teaches that no attempt at concealment might be intended to conceal an infection to catch your man off guard both men had been trained in a harsh and very experienced school Hollywood would have been surprised

R&D called having the hots for

# blahcoover

## I

I saw you eating in a parking, lot, god-given gaydar She stopped, stooped with feet
planted, and rubbed her cigarette out on the hardscrabble sidewalk in an abstract
expressionist gesture 4-7 Columbian Joe Mother's voice I'm lazy and selfish beau-
coup horsemen ghost wowsville world cafe a historical darl going non-native
wannabe married couple church parade ninety-nine times around the block now a
rounder a bad case of the same thing gal Loon so much mileage out of a gas tank
shift of meaning shaftette shag a chapel from person to place 2 all about sound
foreign language snippets of music for concert assassin nowsville is so yesterday
but u.k. spears lives in their highschool neighbourhood MWK2M dr. husband go it
alone why his hatred fear of cops equals no society but the aesthetic trump card lis-
ten to phone he doesn't like being looked at women's restrained voices life not in
service millenial when my man picks up trash he puts it in the garbage getting a lot
of yardage out of that *aild* yes anti-joyce's empty affirmation description bulge guns
chalk line passing the gas station signs urban eyes *moderne* titty bars *I recognized*
*the book before you* did I recognized? thirty years old before you get in a fight what
kind of cowboy are you? Mohammed Refi's *if I saw it* on tv I'd laugh out loud but it's
the way I feel right now *YLT* from Black to blue chase the scene Bernard in black face
statesman then = "must say nothing shots in hotel room alt.bedroom she – arches –
he – classical" perspectival interior mall to victory I don't like being I know honey I
know look sewing machines like a tv commercial fingers Harvey Keitel if you know
you can do it you can do it it's, just like limping she's not be-bop mister still carpet-
fool as unmanageable add E hate children looking her gaze moral shoulder holster

RENTAL

driving his cars at me words shape to fill a lack close of dream book the devil ill who doesn't understand erasing white/black bond *i.e.* will write I went erase went to the store *i.e.* her gaps computer writing it down versus computer writing beige cover punk band the sex pistols have a good and are making they're would be looking at *fabergé* pint hotel *qué séra séra* domestic if you don't know you can do it my american neighbours wear a proud to be canadian digital t-shirt it's just like limping D.D. – lookout angel of the morning i learned in africa the school is a dark brighter than the continent of vancouver island I'll stop when you stop way h.k. commie's in rinse job prefab sprocket playing during a collection – his fucking infernal eternal cockiness – what's the matter with you, you had the far, *tu* hold the fort eyes are moving all the time all over like seagulls use for a killer jug night Warn her brother's wind'em-up louis loses his Ryan O'Neill sig shore prod to call ultimate white looking lecher cops "burn" line between curtain files stained couch way listens to classical and do-wop crew's shadows long winter one's proctology exam onto[*], phylo, how not depends.

on belief of lovers I don't need anybody putting any doubt in my mind how goth is that you're understood by your relations each G is a im/de/re/o/ex/pression hauled his gun out of the ashes tastes of necessity hashish like reading a stock dictionary loose talk maybe he should get my paycheque knows G.W.F. Hegel but not the blues concussion of syncopation Hughes confuses jazz & house it go win did a little lite fingerwipe dusting the first no not the first you ever saw miss piggy sings same song i dear Lear did to *Oh, God II*'s partner's VW Rabbit board's theory beyond so that's another I don't know what

## II

How is dear Missus Lee?

Bine, multi tumescent. E in boot cherry, fast Che.

I beg your pardon, dear?

*shouting's* trig- End fast Che in boot cherry! writing writing verse writing it down
down or writing writing verse writing it down or writing writing verse writing it or
writing writing verse writing or writing writing verse or writing writing or writing
cause he probably figures I'd tell him his life's worth more than a paycheque but
said much after the fact & for a camera for the poem no it was actually for a cam-
era even if it isn't in the film er, in the poem but it is in a poem no it isn't watch
out you don't use closure in your opening arguments that's a big no-no you cocks
can just suck my musical hoop ride beaucoup de horsemen

## III

I go for a man who
doesn't sneeze for a living
like that offers it self
up to you makes you
want to have an
allergy sneeze smashes one
octopus in a 3 tvs per household
legged kilt race rule book by
the really rottens like rock get out
of the moustache house of
hate & into my shoes
I want every under
cover covered, one
hundred per scent
after blowing on a record
while you're sweepin'
we're a sleepin' air bubble
shipper go mister condo indie
rock semi alcoholic drama
queen ruined her christmas
she didn't get sound enthusiastic
but he took some southern comfort
at her apartment behind the strip
plaza in the she had not felt
enthusiasm about anything
in a year improvised log

R
E
N
T
A
L

confetti like to retire
into an underground
house that wouldn't
that commercial sells its
elf superioristic tone
how the machinations
attached to the most
routine acts, like
making a telephone call
or answering a doorbell
child finding rolls of quarters
west coast architecture
in the gulf war snaphots how
cammo works for the
colourblind death row sketches
scissor lift head brace
man from mars in 80-81
tubby one's one overall
strap's dangling brolly
the outside of
a two story and die of
try fucking she could
not get rid of the we
want a place to preach not to piss
fine as wine I blew cold "wind" down my
upper lip. No dice. OK scratch that.

## IV

laundry room door latch
underneath a sink
as if sleeping
pulled out make-up baskets
make-up for girls make-up for dolls
*a cross of lotion on a mirror,* sparkles
the rat lifted slowly
black goo underneath
an inside out
white plastic bag
turned inside out
coffin
liner

# V

*hi* shit eating grin
rats short of
*wascally wabbit*
but
dean is death
his eat
record
not much not
like that roto rooter
truck passing by
hose in nose

# Flower Daddy Haiku

son's lie LAX 127 buds
sake bottle perfume
oh lost romance!

sung lilacs
perfume pair
is contrast

topiary
secateurs

cherry blossom petals
stroller wheels
miss *M\*A\*S\*H*

son's lilac
127 Bud lites
Vaisaki bottle
oh, lost romance!

petals
sting
face blurning wind

flou
[as in flour
her
s$_c$ent

## I Have a Third Grade Sense of Humor
## (Rental Van 4.1)

uh    toy    son
this one's for all the I got killer slugs in my $100 Joe Foreman grillers
the tongue model, bootin' it down
bollywood so's to fuck up
cultural lag so punk

like    but YOU
were THERE
the LIGHT to fuck up the snick

fence gate as Ginger from D.O.A.
six thousand dick bullfrog

tetris urine male,

poo drilled pee thru clear plastic alien's head
for clerihews as clerical errors read seventies marxist-structuralists

cell plant right there
penis open    field's been there done what
*hippies survived Nixon punks didn't survive Reagan haha
are you taking over or are you taking orders

how Mark Laba of hat is his
a discourse future
bad i.e. sixties were wrong
swords i.e. so excited they were speaking english

unlice-      history: how to show
before *Star Wars*, what time was (      ) reagan*

like rocker took over poetry
the      that bodies
age linear, their youngsters play their mentors

nail clippers to tear the water bottle neck
is      throw the baby out with
the bathwater as Adorno as trust fund kid

italian dinosaur in italian versus
Sammy Davis, Jr. jawlines
URL on their fleece vest versus Wall Street's
last detail      men

2 a.m. fire crackers after voices & magazines click

spiderman and batman and reagan bush suh
on a warm day the top
beer can warms up      bottom's still
cold is proficient not a problem

Yogi Berra in a guayabera
the bottom's still cold

it's fucking ... fecking ... hi my name is guinevere
it's fucking cold in here
wash your vagina here      *Thriller*
limo stroller

with my bullshit attitude jew
quoted in the ovaltine
how hard it is to tell

rat poison


jails


you have no unheard messages
fail his defence loans

americanism how do you
wedding? Cement truck! as anti-    not anti-

weasel     ating her fries like fingers
you     the monkey? children

flight from modernity the drivers cooling their

left elbows     anorexic on a smartie utterance
ide via


trenches where real speech takes
name is M=U=D

happy sadsack voice        to hell
that's what Pavement on the answering machine'll getcha

Telcom's atlantic ultimate team or ultimate team atlantic picks?
like a        replacement piss
equisetum =        green siouxie hairdos
nude white    soda


double dabber
soup & fish


Hey guess what?
What? i just learned you can't chew
Great!
Did you hear fucking word I said?
Yeah you said you've got a jones in
your bag


to be called multi-
get in the fucking west
not you!?

got any rigs? darlings
new     cardlock get your
not just     also
about

there's more beer in the stroller (manifest content)
sure american her shorthand his short hand (   )

denial not    not    back in the
ound the
old school was new school lite

pink god's gift to world men
tush went to your     o whip
trash can with more holes than afghan
your     head wall flapgate structure

my jubilee's over effortless & emo-phobic
plays    old navy digital
trance to venial sin navel rose her hawaii

to idea
express amazement through babyfood jar pressed espresso

then    not    of

and then? and then? and then? and then?
equals mountain love which, in fact, it does

                                                if not
               to colour     but the brightness of
           plastic under cali sun outer space
                          i let myself in, hope


                               water to the anal
                   must of a regard front the of
         locked better than monkeywrench to

go it's funny seeing three goths in sunshine
                   talk to a mauve haltertop
                              and jeans ford


                            sorry did mean I
       mean        left behind on the mill
           crawl of      mall walk of  if
                    meaning is working
who's the cutman in your corner? only
                          women venn


         spanish: agundo     pregnant
       fight fan –is –on. –is –on. –is –on.


              if you learn    you learn                R
                                                       E
                                                       N
       her breasts    removed? of cold                 T
     beer on it. drink the applejack made              A
            smell is      smell   smell is             L

that just shows to go you
neighbours    thrill
pornographic memory
blackouts as autobiography
motivated, really

that's quite a chunk of mazuma!
shut up
said not meaning it
chuck-a-lu    bernie

what's that in aid of dead mackeral:
so much grease
from the goose goes
down the drain panama canal's
a busy
ditch stop digging my
graveside manner
with my

fine print for less time
makes
me wonder

poets than

page 12    's female    which f-word I
any fag stabbed the dark

for the umpteenth time if
million times for
the first time in my life i was
genuinely scared i heard
for the life of me draw a picture
of her looked

over the head of practicing anti-terrorist unit
she searched for
her keys,     sticking her hands
in her skintight jeans, pulling     i'll
take first downs on'er he frowned

people     deaf     cigarettes
whose?
carefully?

so I repeated myself again
pulled away
ya cleaning car     =     her ejaculation

relationship between
no cells at work rule & general oppression (none)

Bravo Zulu grip and grins're required
but you can move some to next week.

*VANCOUVER-BROOKLYN 5/02-1/03*

R
E
N
T
A
L

## Poverty Pimp

following pages document six
. In this time period
Can, can, can-can, First
Much of this would

disagree with each other
encouraging them to do
often did occasion good
poetry, what's the use

interesting for me to
other disenfranchised people. I
rewarding work from my
*human context for observations*

detoxed from heroin 20
to say more than
life as a checker
fixing's in an Altoid's

California".[1] "Spring and
only read light stuff
a very enthusiastic speaker
Native stories? IE taping/interviewing

He'd had some attitude
to cut him out
girlfriend o.d.'ing the next
series of statements we

about the blood-stained maple
to read [or be
my brain was frozen
of the street, "greasy".

to be rude dude
class entering their poems
Haida art on the
better at blocking out

not to single out
meanings associated with words
he liked the dissecting
generals' helicopter was shot

English from watching *Star*
wasn't just blowing smoke
*as the Hep C*
habit – down to 28

"*province of the pimp*
commodification & marketability aspects

Rosez, A. Badger aka
hangers-on with poor literacy

Aren't You Tired of
Larry C on Laba
better than he expected
simple in its description

had to go *up*town,
workers will be lonely
depressing anecdotes about "w-h-o-r-e-s"
Albert Camus via Algeria],

there was a boxer
"sally ann"'s a Canadianism
Wanky, an African guy
same porn different storm

R
E
N
T
A
L

# Choke the Chicken Hawk Leftist

*for Dorothy*

*and each year? I'm pouring out more beer for deceased peers*

                              CB:
Name your price.

                              DT:
shows up in reverse diaspora narratives as voicd

                              CB:
calculator

                              DT:
woman with sushi tattoo buys a mr noodle, goes to work at red hot video: so
much for direct action

                              CB:
anarchy only works if you don't have kids but are one

                              DT:
isn't supposed to work, you dingbat!

CB:

praise for how she handles *oral tragedy*: vote with your throat memory, not cope

*(pause)*

who told who to read slower

DT:

no, who told *whom* to read slower. i was wondering when you'd work him in. glass ceiling depends on how you spell it

CB:

*poets* who *had* kids *before* their *careers* started *versus* poets *who* had *kids* after *their* careers *started* versus *poets* with *no* kids *versus* poets *with* no *careers* versus *poets* with *neither*

DT:

the problem with trying to use cultural capital to accumulate political or economic capital is that the cultural is the affect of the economic (as is the political?): it's like acting drunk to try and get drunk, ain't gonna work, poverdetermination is a two-way street and you still can't go backwards.

CB:

sro-chic, woodwards –

DT:

sure, go ahead. don't say i didn't.

CB:

blind

DT:

blinders

CB:

bling bling

DT:

we already went through that . . . don't give a shit and a shake.

CB:

We walked to the mouth of the alley. Just shy of . . . yay high. In the mirror, she looks Iranian.

DT:

What are you doing with a dead cop's penis.

CB:

Busta rhymes with trust fund. That's because you're not listening.

DT:

The *transgendered* person handles that automatic like she was born in Flatbush. Also: Billy Barty as pool player. Video your paintball crimes.

CB:

The american ex-businessman wearing "yellow measuring tape" suspenders, floral ball cap, driving a white stretch SUV, *The Seven Pillars of Wisdom* open on the dash. Unmarked police car with trunk open, no one around.

# Chicken Fallujah

*for Chris Stroffolino*

marine screams the new dark meet me at the anime next to the labour ready

cottage sit-ups and spin dustryuse

how is that puppy doin'?

two a.m. feeding at a house away from the Pier 1 imports and tim horton drive
thru tree a 16 oz. cup on a truck up on blocks topsoil for sale the dalai nambla in
canada the pope in mexico

if magnets are our sexuality and superglue the supermax of late mucilage why do
fridge magnets end up obscuring the surface of our food's daddy
(mommy?)(womb?) like PMC advisory stickers do the already too small CD art
well, because sometimes when mommy and i are watching a video and we hear
you we pause it and one of us comes in to see if you're alright is why

early evening
the clatter of dishes
beeps of microwave buttons
a story and a yard away
mommy scissors

mommy stickers
mommy seizures
mommy sees hers
the horror or the joy are too intense to distance from write about

puppies on strings *scratch that* i mean pussies on strings
come on kitty
mouthes shaped like anuses to make the kiss sound loud enough
Devon's sketches in my notebook miro-like

two LED screen on clothing
capitalalia
muthafuckalalia
mattealaia
umbertoalalia
genitorturealia
genitalalia

what do you mean
*if i just lie in bed*
my parents are the
parents ~~my~~ their
parents warned
me ~~them~~
about etc

urge overlalia
over you are elle alalia

U R L alalia

worried if it's revenge of the nerd
or rudolph the red nose ranger-scapegoat
situation
know what I'm sayin?
was she good looking?
yeah she was good looking


the march long weekend through the institutions
williams plus mao times the recycling bin of history
divided by there aint no n-word like a mississipi nigga
equals no one gets a job – everyone agrees the nineties were a period of econom-
ic determinism – that's why the art was so good
and the poetry so shitty
it streaked porcelain
//////////////////////////////////////////////////////////////////////////
//////////////////////////////////////////////////////////////////////////
//// cowboys moyou ve through towns like cossacks, comanche actor in Hudson's
Bay blanket . . . it's hard to believe they're white, they aint white, anymore


maybe you can help us all white, all captive, there's the white girl there


father puts the letter next to his penis from grow *up* to *grow* op to grow rip


chief looks like fonzie . . . the notorious C.B.


MY evil empire includes

the sunny ellipsoid
steering club cultures
toward a late bus that
remembering the first
articulated bus you rode to
the sub in the early 90s
becomes a every bus
serial airport haggling
price points with the Betty
Ford Clinic piss campus
But Y Dad Y

if mount pleasant
is a market that
you have to go up the
hill to go down the W
because SUV's cut off
men w/ walkers
that's why wallet chains
getting stuck in bus stop
benches so only truckers
who never take the bus
the street cleaner who
in paradise is either
unionized or on community
service has stars of
david on one sleeve
the crescent on the

R
E
N
T
A
L

other and an orange
safety vest on
I can see the wires
in the safety glass ceiling
but not
clearly too pick up
trucks two trailers
nine porta potties
the screen in their ventilation
holes in the roof flophouse
disk softcore money
hard meteres a word
b word d word e word
g word h word i word  ·
j word k word l word
m word o word p word
q word r word s word
t word u word v word
w word x word y word
zed word
street scholar

fake vintage heavy metal T's
recall an era of chains
whipped on freshly nailed
tabletops – zippers, cutlery

feminem on the fm not

play the str8 & proud for
you my amigo put the
amway lingo on layaway so
as to . . . EI is a cash
cow for us the lobbying
brought the corporate tax rape
down to rustbeltafarian

who did Clint want? redlegs?

Texicans that'll be the day
became Buddy's hit

stop the man from stopping the man

rag hat, blanket head
eye-evacuator
tasselled loafer rifle case

from pioneer shack to
post-industrial trailer trash

cops do script run thru

K-POO scratchy records

poetry as company picnic
I'm a jew jew kind of jew

R
E
N
T
A
L

oooooooooooooooooooooooooooooooo
OoOoOoOoOoOoOoOoOoOoOoOoOo

Don Ameche reference

wanna bust'em picking
your feet in poughkeepsie

if time was an 8-track pretzelsandwich
clock radio from flipping to digital

LCD vs LED vs DVD vs CEO

triple dot/dog man darkness

radio makes it hard to blend

Godzilla this is the life
you're lucky if you got 2 kinds of life

teaching as time-release capsule

contractor fired for taking pix
of coffins (stars to left) vs teenager
crying in soccer field of headstones

Queenking no park
pocket is no silence for peace

Pottery Barn marks start of the Castro

the Yuma

choose your prison

ever stop to think & forget to *start* again?

just say Mo

event security for 9/11

god can do anything but fail

ok other car other car
AM cop to WF cop while cuffing
BF I can do it on the way back

*DPT* you don't have to be one of them
73% of women think they have damaged hair

Range Rover plate: ERRANDS

R
E   knee splint why guy leather man in shorts
N   across from the Levi-Strauss museum
T
A   girl in tube top runs out of church &
L   gets into a car (her parents)

Ralph Garcia jiu-jitsu
parents are anti-drugs
make art not obey make war

ahistorical girl on longboard clutches
ahistorical girl on mustang banana seat
= string around neck of great dane

rolling stone cycle trike helmet corners
continual conversation

JDUBZ why uma thurman doesn't love me
she doesn't know me
she's never met me
she will never meet me
she's never heard of me
she's taken

arranges coffins w/ uses music to punish
uses punishment to deter
uses used cars to calm down drive time

fuck vic chesnutt ctrl-alt-country
where's the red neck pillow

ever wake up with a quarter in your hand
and hair in your mouth?
sorry I forgot to pay you

the shyness compensates for the schmoozing

no hippies just a lot of higher prices

phone card posters
and you've reached Bernstein

hands-off parenting

she had some other things too some white things
crawling I think they were lice

manicurist picks up alley garbage w/ bare hands

money talks bullshit walks
take the money & starve

black crackers

you'll love the Haight

I was, I am 13 months in 'n'
13 months out girl, girl
I was back to back
you do that then you
can tell me about
13 in then 13 out

R
E
N
T
A
L

YES I WANT A CORPORATE BRIBE LEXUS
gangbangers w/ laptop in Benz

I got my own back

beard w/ short hair = Beat

let freedom ring
there got to be limits to ringtones

high as fuck off

not a genuine white man

kelly-green barracuda 383 about to be towed

one of the things for gender roles 101
is ground rules for conversation

yeah more stead, hunh
not finding it's fresh

I tell you I get my cheque
on the twenty-*eight*
I always get my cheque *ear*ly
man I tell you

*SAN FRANCISCO-VANCOUVER* April 2004

R
E
N
T
A
L

# Acknowledgments

"super proximity chairs med pep dunk tank" was first published in the <u>Queen Street Review</u>

"di da di" and "Chicken Fallujah" were first published in <u>W</u>

"A.M.I.I.C.A.F." was first published in <u>West Coast Line</u>

"inverted -V" was first stapled to Mount Pleasant telephone poles

"MP Haiku" were mailed one at a time to Gerry Gilbert in March 2001

"gotta lexander gumbo Itsuky galeh angus lark" was first published in <u>unarmed</u>

"Choke the Chicken Haute Leftist" was first published in a Dorothy Trujillo Lusk <u>festschrift</u>

## ABOUT THE AUTHOR

Clint Burnham was born in Comox, British Columbia in 1962. He attended university at Royal Roads Military College, the University of Victoria, and York University. Clint has taught at the University of British Columbia, Capilano College, Emily Carr Institute, and for three years ran an outreach program in Vancouver's Downtown Eastside. His short story collection *Airborne Photo* was at the centre of a sexual harrassment case at a Vancouver college, and his novel *Smoke Show* was shortlisted for a B.C. Book Prize in 2006.